Autumne Burks

New York Times Bestselling Author

ANDY ANDREWS

capturing life's greatest gifts

The PERFECT MOMENT

THOMAS NELSON
Since 1798

Published in Nashville, Tennessee, by Thomas Nelson. Thomas Nelson is a registered trademark of HarperCollins Christian Publishing, Inc.

Photo Credits
Cover: Design Pics/Thinkstock; Özgür Donmaz/Thinkstock; Sergey Mironov/Thinkstock; sirandel/Thinkstock; Vernon Wiley/Thinkstock; Andy Andrews; NuConcept/Shutterstock
Internals: page 1, Design Pics/Thinkstock; Özgür Donmaz/Thinkstock; Sergey Mironov/Thinkstock; sirandel/Thinkstock; Vernon Wiley/Thinkstock; Andy Andrews; NuConcept/Shutterstock; page 2, Apostrophe/Shutterstock; page 3, Christy Mouery Haynes/BeachChicPhotography.com; page 4, Oleg Golovnev/Shutterstock, javarman/Shutterstock; page 6, pashabo/Shutterstock, 100ker/Shutterstock; pages 8–9, Galyna Andrushko/Shutterstock; pages 10–11, javarman/Shutterstock, sergign/Shutterstock; page 13, christian keller/Thinkstock; pages 14–15, Olga Khoroshunova/123RF; pages 20–21, Warren Goldswain/Shutterstock; pages 22–23, javarman/Shutterstock; pages 24–25, Greenview/Shutterstock; page 27, Elena Elisseeva/123RF; page 29, Piotr Wytrazek/Shutterstock; page 30–31, David Polite/Shutterstock; page 34–35, Zurijeta/Shutterstock; page 38, BarracudaDesigns/Shutterstock; page 41, Christy Mouery Haynes/BeachChicPhotography.com; pages 46–47, Christy Mouery Haynes/BeachChicPhotography.com; page 48, Helen Hotson/Shutterstock; page 53, Helen Hotson/Shutterstock; page 59, Alhovik/Shutterstock; pages 60–61, Dudarev Mikhail/Shutterstock; pages 62–63, Christy Mouery Haynes/BeachChicPhotography.com; pages 66–67, Andrey tiyk/Shutterstock; pages 74–75, Andrey tiyk/Shutterstock; page 77, Christy Mouery Haynes/BeachChicPhotography.com; pages 86–87, Efired/Shutterstock; pages 90–91, Christy Mouery Haynes/BeachChicPhotography.com; pages 92–93, spirit of america/Shutterstock; page 94, Willyam Bradberry/Shutterstock

Thomas Nelson titles may be purchased in bulk for educational, business, fund-raising, or sales promotional use. For information, please e-mail SpecialMarkets@ThomasNelson.com.

ISBN-13: 978-0-7180-3261-6

Printed in China
15 16 17 18 19 20 TIMS 6 5 4 3 2 1

STOP.

Just for a moment.

Look around. Are you alone?

Even if there are people nearby . . .

are you alone right now?

To be certain, this is an odd beginning to our time together, but I have no real "action" to grab you and focus your thoughts. Yet, your complete and undivided attention is needed for less than five minutes. And if you dare spend the time . . . these five minutes will change your life.

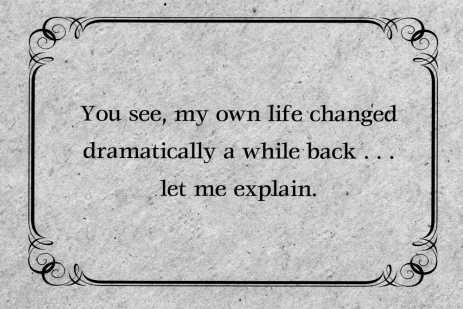

You see, my own life changed
dramatically a while back . . .
let me explain.

I was sitting in a porch swing on a dock watching Austin, my eight-year-old boy, as he fished. He was barefoot and wore nothing but shorts and a T-shirt. It was late afternoon, and I was tired, having worked since early morning, but I was aware that I was comfortable.

Now understand: I am not often "conscious" of comfort. Oh sure, I know when my socks are wet or when my back hurts, but I never seem to notice when my socks are dry or when my back *doesn't* hurt.

Anyway, my son talked and fished, and I became strangely tuned in to the fact that I did not have a headache, I wasn't hungry or thirsty, a cool breeze was in my face, and I had nothing in particular pressing with my schedule. There was nowhere I had to be, no one I needed to call.

As I look back,

it was indeed a peculiar feeling

that only foreshadowed the moment

that was about to change me forever.

Austin talked as he tied the hook on his line. He told me the bait was squid and that if he didn't wash his hands, he would be able to let the kids in his class smell it tomorrow.

He laughed and so did I.

After a few minutes of not catching anything, he said, "The reason I like to fish is because when everything is still and quiet, your whole self is full of hoping. And whether you catch anything or not, you get to hope. It's a great feeling, isn't it? Hope, I mean. It's next best to excitement."

I agreed that it was.

The sun was sinking low over the water when he said, "Dad? Let's throw the football."

"Okay," I answered and eased out of the swing as my boy hurried past me, rushing to stow his fishing gear and get the ball. His feet hammered loudly on the old boards of the dock.

"Stand over there," he directed as I moved onto the beach, "and I'll stand here. That way the sun won't be in either of our faces."

For several minutes we passed the ball back and forth in silence. Then he said, "I'm going long."

"Go!" I answered and he turned, running hard and away, all elbows and knees as I arched the ball high into the air.

It spiraled perfectly, hanging that tiny bit at the top of its flight, then settling softly over my son's left shoulder as he caught it and fell dramatically onto the sand.

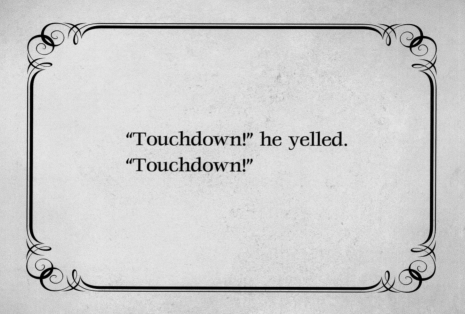

"Touchdown!" he yelled.
"Touchdown!"

He sat up as I stepped toward him and motioned for the ball. Smiling, he held out his hand and said, "Dad! Stop!"

I did.

"Do you see?" he asked.

I raised my eyebrows and quickly looked around. "What?" I replied.

"Look!" he insisted as he got to his feet and came closer. He grinned widely, and I chuckled as I noticed the gap where his two front teeth used to be.

"Dad, don't you see?" he said again, and I shook my head, mystified.

"No," I told my boy. I did not see.

He took my right hand in both of his.

"Well," he began, "think about it . . . The sun went down, so it's not in anybody's eyes, but it is still light enough to throw the football. The sand is soft enough to fall on, and the temperature is not too hot and it's not too cold."

He shrugged. "And it's just you and me here together."

Pausing, he looked at me earnestly.

"Dad," he said,
"it's just perfect."

And it was.

As I sit here today in what the world calls the "middle-aged" years of my life, it occurs to me that I have existed for decades on this planet. And I have managed to notice every cross word or disappointed glance tossed my way.

For years, I have paid close attention to hurricanes forming in the Caribbean. I've spent hours captivated by news coverage about fires, earthquakes, floods, and tornadoes.

I have slowed down to see wrecks on the highway.

I see every bill that comes in the mail. I mark every flight that is delayed. I even see the spot on my car's fender that was missed when it was washed.

I have paid attention to things that weren't true. I have wasted time on things with no lasting significance. And I have worried about things that never happened.

Oh God, how many moments have I missed that were just perfect?

I want to live a happy life, one for which I am grateful and acutely aware of time well spent.

From this day forward, I will notice the joy on a child's face, not the chocolate he left on the couch.

I will notice clean sheets, the roof over my head, and the fact that I have enough to eat. I will see opportunities to help or to teach and be grateful for my life.

And though I will continue to question and grow and struggle and learn, I know now that I must never again let a special moment pass without acknowledging, at least to myself, that . . .

"Wow!

This . . . right here,

right now . . . is just perfect!"

CREATING
YOUR
PERFECT
MOMENTS

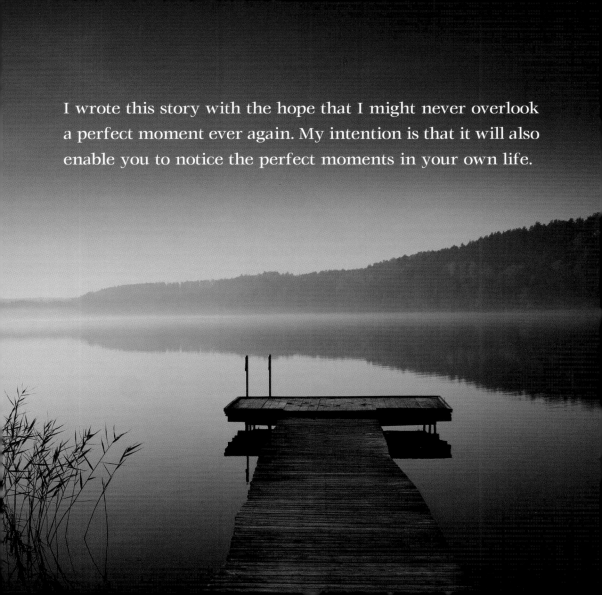

I wrote this story with the hope that I might never overlook a perfect moment ever again. My intention is that it will also enable you to notice the perfect moments in your own life.

But I also know that noticing these moments is not always as easy as it sounds. After all, it took me more than forty years before I was aware enough to notice the one you just read!

The goal is not only to never miss a perfect moment again, but also to become intentional about creating an atmosphere that is conducive to perfect moments—not just for yourself, but for the ones you love, as well.

As a side note, please know that when I use the word *perfect*, I am using it loosely. We all know that the true definition of perfection is simply not attainable. The true definition of perfection is an impossible standard to hold ourselves to and can often end up being an unhealthy practice.

So, for the purposes of this book, let's settle on the definition of *perfect* as "the best something can possibly be." We are out to create moments that are as good as they can be, lives as good as they can be, and ourselves . . . as good as we can be.

Perfect:

The best something can possibly be

Stop waiting for contentment, comfort, and happiness. The reality is . . . *they* are the ones waiting for *you*.

THE
PERFECT
INGREDIENTS

Take a little bit of time to think and reflect deeply about your "perfect moments."

The first step is to determine the ingredients necessary for a perfect moment to take place. I jotted down what was important to me:

HEALTH—I am physically well enough to enjoy basic activities.

FAMILY—My wife, Polly, or one of my two sons, Austin and Adam, is there to share the moment with me.

COMFORT—No small ache or pain, like a headache or a sore back, is distracting me from the moment.

OPEN SCHEDULE—Nothing is pressing on my calendar. I am focused on nothing else and am 100 percent present in the moment.

Wow! It is astonishing for me to look at that list and realize that those four things are all I need to have a truly perfect moment. I would venture to guess that those four ingredients come together at least once a week, even when I'm busy. And yet it took me more than forty years to notice one of these weekly moments.

The really great thing about this list, however, is that even if you take away one of those ingredients, the outcome is still a highly enjoyable moment.

Remember, things don't have to be perfect for you to be happy.

For instance, let's say I'm healthy, completely comfortable, and enjoying a nice dinner with my wife, but I happen to have a deadline coming up in a day or two. That deadline may be in the back of my mind somewhere, but that does not have to stop me from focusing on enjoying a meal with the woman I love.

Sometimes we set up so many rules for how things need to be for us to have perfect moments. But if you go back to basics and focus on what really matters, you may find it's not as hard as you think to be happy every day.

IMAGINE THAT!

THE
RIGHT
PERSPECTIVE

Right now, there are perfect moments occurring in your life, no matter how bad things may seem.

THE PERFECT MOMENT

Without the right perspective, your list of perfect moment ingredients isn't going to do a whole lot for you.

For example, in my book *The Noticer*, I recount a real memory of a meal I shared with Jones, the book's central character. He had invited me to join him on a sand dune near the ocean for what he called a "feast." This "feast" turned out to be Vienna sausages and sardines. As we began the meal, he asked me what I was eating.

Puzzled, and a little annoyed by what the "feast" had turned out to be, I said, "I'm eating sardines and Vienna sausages." "Where?" he responded. Still annoyed, I answered, "In the sand."

He responded with something
extraordinary that still affects
me to this day:

"Young man, you see only the sand at your feet and what you are eating, which you wish was something else. I don't tell you this as a rebuke; you are very ordinary in your views. Most people are just like you, disgusted with themselves for what they are and what they eat and what they drive. Most of us never stop to think that there are quite literally millions in this world who lack our blessings and opportunities, have no food to eat at all, and no hope of ever owning a car."

Then, he really hit me with something: "Incidentally, *you* ate sardines and Vienna sausages in the sand. *I* dined on surf and turf with an ocean view. It's all about perspective."

A great exercise in perspective is to make a list of the things you often take for granted. Here's my list:

1. Shelter
2. Easy access to transportation
3. Healthy family
4. Good memories
5. The freedom my country provides
6. A good community in which to raise my boys
7. Past mistakes—they made me stronger

What do you often take for granted in your life?

When Jones shared his sardines and Vienna sausages with me, I was homeless, alone, and bitter toward the world. But I had my health. I had freedom. I had plenty of good memories (but I chose to focus on the bad ones). And he was right—I even had an ocean view! I just needed a little shift in my perspective to realize those things.

CREATING YOUR PERFECT MOMENTS

Once you start noticing your life's perfect moments, there is only one thing you are going to want to do—create them intentionally.

You see, I didn't set out to create that perfect moment between Austin and me. It just happened on its own. And, most of the time, that's how perfect moments are going to happen. I mean, how many times have you planned an afternoon with your family or friends that you thought was going to be perfect, only for some unforeseen interruption or setback to derail the whole occasion?

LIFE, AS THEY SAY, RARELY GOES ACCORDING TO PLAN.

So, if planning perfect moments rarely works, how can we go about creating more of them? It's simple: we create an environment conducive to perfect moments. The first step is to determine what this environment looks like.

These three questions will get you started!

What excites you more than anything else?

 What people do you particularly enjoy being around?

 If this were your last day, what would you do?

Based on your responses to these three questions, it's pretty easy to see the type of environment where most of your perfect moments would occur.

After answering these questions, you may also find that your current life situation and your perfect moment environment are not aligned. It could be that the beach excites you more than anything else, but you live in a high-rise in the city. Or maybe a relationship just ended with the person you want to be around and love the most.

Look at the circumstances of your life: What's holding you back, and what can you do?

From Perfect Moments
to an Incredible Life

So how do we go from perfect moments to an incredibly fulfilling life? We start by figuring out exactly where we are. Let's do that by focusing on what happened within the last year. There is a reason we're starting with gratitude.

In my book *The Traveler's Gift*, I explain how happiness comes from gratitude. It is tough for the seeds of depression to take root in a truly grateful heart. Coming from this place, you may see the past year from a different perspective.

Here are some thoughts to get you started.

<u>Over the Past Year:</u>

1. The experience I've been most grateful for is . . .
2. The person I've been most grateful for is . . .
3. The lesson I've been most grateful for is . . .
4. The moment when I was most passionate and excited about my life was when . . .
5. The best memory I created was when . . .
6. The skill I've gained that I will need most going forward is . . .
7. My proudest accomplishment was when . . .

8. The thing that has robbed me of the most time and energy has been . . .

9. I would have enjoyed life 100 percent more if I had only . . .

10. My loved ones would have better known my love if I had only . . .

11. The world would have seen the difference I could have made if I had only . . .

12. If I could change one thing it would be . . .

The way you completed those statements should give you a good idea of where you are in your life today. You may feel disappointed, scared, excited, hopeful, or any number of emotions.

IF YOU'RE WORRIED, DON'T BE—YOU'RE ABOUT TO CREATE A VISION FOR A LIFE THAT YOU LOVE.

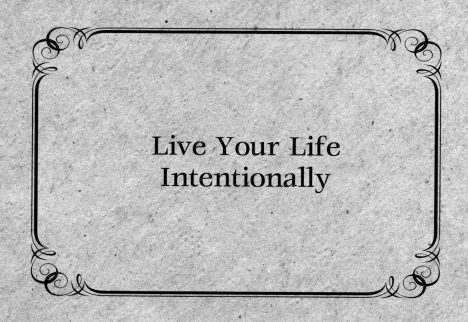

Live Your Life
Intentionally

Let's create some desired outcomes for the next six months so that you can live your life intentionally.

When we live intentionally, we are able to create the future we want for our lives. By visualizing, writing, and taking small steps toward what you want, you can create a positive shift. Change can happen instantly!

Review each of these statements and develop a template of what you want the next six months to look like.

Over the Next Six Months:

1. I will no longer let this hold me back . . .
2. If I want to make myself and my loved ones feel better, the first thing I will STOP doing is . . .
3. My family relationships will improve because . . .
4. My professional life will be focused on . . .
5. I will be financially secure enough to . . .
6. My best moment will be when I . . .
7. I will be happy that I took the time to . . .
8. I will bring joy to everyone around me by . . .
9. The one word I will bring to people's minds is . . .
10. I will write a letter telling these five people how much of a difference they have made in my life . . .

11. I will be able to sum up my life by saying . . .
12. If I knew I would not fail, the first thing I would do is . . .
13. If I wanted to revive an old dream I'd given up on,
    I would . . .
14. I will celebrate by . . .
15. I will begin to fulfill my purpose, which is to . . .

Follow Through

Do you have a better idea of where your life is now and where you want to take it? Are you excited? You can take your life down any path you choose. You can choose to be open and available to creating perfect moments every day, which in turn lead to living an incredible and fulfilling life.

Let's review the steps:

1. **The Perfect Ingredients:** What do I need for a perfect moment to take place?
2. **The Right Perspective:** How can I see things differently?
3. **Creating Perfect Moments:** What is my favorite environment?
4. **Envisioning the Incredible Life:** How can I live each day intentionally?

Let's take it one step further. To really accomplish everything you want for the next six months of your life, you must take action. What are you going to do? Who are you going to call? What meeting are you going to set up immediately? What can you do *TODAY*?

This is not the time to lose steam! Take a few more moments to write down what you're going to do, and give each action a deadline. And, if you want to be held accountable, share these three action steps with someone you trust.

1. The first thing I will do to ensure the next six months are outstanding is . . .

_____

_____

_____

_____

_____

_____

_____

_____

_____

_____

COMPLETION DATE: _____

2. The second thing I will do to ensure the next six
   months are outstanding is . . .

_____

_____

_____

_____

_____

_____

_____

_____

_____

_____

COMPLETION DATE: _____

3. The third thing I will do to ensure the next six months are outstanding is . . .

_____

_____

_____

_____

_____

_____

_____

_____

_____

COMPLETION DATE: _____

WHERE YOU GO FROM HERE

Ultimately, the direction of your life is up to one person—you.

Do not let outside influences sway or determine your vision. Continue to take purposeful action with every day that passes. Though your path will be fraught with difficulty, the rewards of living your life intentionally will far outweigh the cost.

Do more than is required of you. Aim higher than others. Laugh a bit more than the joke deserved. Be kind and patient when you don't feel like it. Try harder than you did yesterday. Become a "noticer," and be grateful for the things you have overlooked for too long. After all, your next perfect moment could be just around the corner. Don't miss it!

ABOUT
ANDY ANDREWS

Hailed by a *New York Times* reporter as "someone who has quietly become one of the most influential people in America," Andy Andrews is the author of the *New York Times* bestsellers *The Traveler's Gift*, *The Noticer*, and *How Do You Kill 11 Million People?* He is also an in-demand speaker for the world's largest organizations. Zig Ziglar said, "Andy Andrews is the best speaker I have ever seen."

The Traveler's Gift was a featured selection on ABC's *Good Morning America* and continues to appear on bestseller lists around the world. His books have been translated into more than twenty-five languages.

Andy has spoken at the request of four different U.S. presidents, has addressed members of Congress and their spouses, and toured military bases around the world, being called upon by the Department of Defense to speak about the principles contained in his books.

Arguably, there is no person on the planet better at weaving subtle yet life-changing lessons into riveting tales of adventure and intrigue—both on paper and onstage.

He lives in Orange Beach, Alabama, with his wife, Polly, and their two sons.

DOES *My* LIFE REALLY MATTER?

With beautiful artwork and incredible, true storytelling, THE BUTTERFLY EFFECT answers the question people have been asking for centuries.

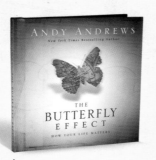

THE BUTTERFLY EFFECT
HOW YOUR LIFE MATTERS
ANDY ANDREWS

You're Invited to *AndyAndrews.com*

Come visit AndyAndrews.com, where you will find tons of **FREE** resources, ebooks, blog posts, and podcast episodes designed to help you create even more *perfect moments*.

FOLLOW ANDY ONLINE: @ANDYANDREWS  FACEBOOK.COM/ANDYANDREWS